T0193678

Nourishing
MIND, BODY, & SPIRIT

A HEALING JOURNEY
TO THE HIGHER SELF

CRYSTAL CASTLE

BALBOA.PRESS
A DIVISION OF HAY HOUSE

Balboa Press books may be ordered through booksellers or by contacting:

Balboa Press
A Division of Hay House
1663 Liberty Drive
Bloomington, IN 47403
www.balboapress.com
1 (877) 407-4847

Because of the dynamic nature of the Internet, any web addresses or links contained in this book may have changed since publication and may no longer be valid. The views expressed in this work are solely those of the author and do not necessarily reflect the views of the publisher, and the publisher hereby disclaims any responsibility for them.

The author of this book does not dispense medical advice or prescribe the use of any technique as a form of treatment for physical, emotional, or medical problems without the advice of a physician, either directly or indirectly. The intent of the author is only to offer information of a general nature to help you in your quest for emotional and spiritual well-being. In the event you use any of the information in this book for yourself, which is your constitutional right, the author and the publisher assume no responsibility for your actions.

Any people depicted in stock imagery provided by Getty Images are models, and such images are being used for illustrative purposes only. Certain stock imagery © Getty Images.

Cover Design: Prudence Makhura
Cover Artwork: Danielle Heythaler
Editing: Healthy Writer's Life Melina Wedin
Photo Credit: Malaika Hilson

Print information available on the last page.

ISBN: 978-1-9822-4537-5 (sc)
ISBN: 978-1-9822-4538-2 (e)

Library of Congress Control Number: 2020905388

Balboa Press rev. date: 03/23/2020

Contents

Nourishing Mind
Realizing Your True Potential

Nourishing Body
Building Your True Potential

Nourishing Spirit
Maintaining Your True Potential

Acknowledgements

There are so many people to whom I am thankful. Without all of them this book would not be possible.

First off, I would like to thank my parents. While they could have done a lot of things differently, they did what they could with the knowledge that they had and to the best of their abilities. I might have grown up knowing some want, but I was never without a roof over my head, clothes to wear or food to eat. We might have eaten a lot of peanut butter and jelly, and more than our fair share of hamburger helper, but we never went hungry.

They also taught me to be strong, to always fight for what is right and not to stand idly by and do nothing. Because of them, I have a very strong work ethic, don't see people by the color of their skin and have a good set of great core values that have driven me to be the person that I am today. Thank you so much for always loving me unconditionally, even if we haven't always seen eye to eye on things. Thanks for also putting up with my crap. I know I wasn't the easiest kid in the world, but I tried my hardest to be someone you could be proud of.

Next up are all my friends. I'm so blessed to have an amazing circle of friends. If I don't name you specifically here, please don't take it as a slight. The people named here were instrumental in helping me along my book writing journey, so I feel they deserve a special mention. I do have an amazing group of friends, who I don't always get to see as often as I would like, but who are always there for me no matter what so I'm thankful for you.

Danielle Heythaler, what can I say about you except that you are quite possibly the best, best friend a gal can have. I am truly grateful for our almost daily missives and our get togethers, even if they're not as frequent as we would like. Without your creativity, I wouldn't have a beautiful work of art for my cover image. You took what was in my head and put it onto a piece of paper and made it beautiful. I'm so blessed to know you and call you my dearest friend. I'm so glad we had a chance to meet and you weren't weirded out by my being so forward in getting to know you better.

Jennifer Rains and Aimee Laux, you two have been an amazing source of inspiration and have been some of my greatest cheerleaders. I treasure our Girls' Night Out Taco Tuesdays so much and am so grateful to have ladies like you in my life. It's always so nice to get together with you and shoot the breeze, laugh like hyenas and just enjoy life. Aimee, because of you, I'll always remember to "grab life by the pu*$y!!"

To Melina Wedin, my editor, you took my jibber jabber and made it into what this book is today. Without your patience and attention to detail, this book would sound like the ravings of a lunatic. To Malaika Hilson, the photographer for my author photo, you took my thoughts about what I wanted and turned them into something grand. Working with you was amazing and I'm grateful that I stumbled onto you, and that you had time to work with me. It's been such a pleasure having you to help me capture images of both myself and my workshops into images that truly express what's going on. To Prudence Makhura, my cover designer, all I can say is WOW. I sent you something that I threw together, the cover image and my fonts and colors and you came back with something so amazing I couldn't believe it. You truly are magical and I'm grateful I came across you.

To Suzy Wraines, my Habit Change Coach, without you this book wouldn't be done now. I struggled with this for years and you helped me to initiate the small steps necessary to get on track to get this done. I am so grateful to you for your inspiration, your laughs and your humor. Thanks for whipping my butt into shape!!

To Jim Carrey, without whom this book would not have been possible. If not for hearing those words you spoke so many years ago that you believe the meaning of life is to love yourself, I would not have made the specific transition that I did to work harder at loving myself. It is because of those words that I am who I am today so I will always be ever grateful.

To Eric Hotchkiss, I want to say thank you for always being there to listen to my ramblings. I'm grateful we got stuck in an office together, and that we got along so well. I'm glad I got to know you, and I appreciate our existential conversations on everything from the meaning of life, to Superheroes, to the best TV shows to watch. Thanks for always making time for me, for listening to me, for trusting me, for laughing with me, for supporting me and for being a great boss. I can honestly say you're the only boss I've had that I've ever really liked.

Last, but certainly not least, thank you so much to Jeff Castle, my knight in shining armor. If not for you, I would not be the person that I am today. When I met you, my life was a mess and you were terrified of me. I thought you were cute and no matter how hard I tried to get you to go out with me, you kept shooting me down. Then that fateful day at Grattan where we got stuck sharing a hotel room, after that we were pretty much glued at the hip. No matter how much I did to try to get rid of you (and try hard I did), you always held on tightly.

I know I've been a mess and a crazy merry-go-round, but no matter how fast or insane the ride got, you held on for dear life. You were the first person to believe in me and because of that, made me start to believe in myself. You gave me something I didn't have in my life, hope. Hope that there was something better, that I could have better, that I could BE better. You made me believe in myself and without you, my life truly wouldn't be what it is today.

You showed me something no one else had in my life, truly unconditional love. I told you all of the crazy stuff in my life, all of the horrors that I had been through, and instead of seeing me as broken, or damaged goods to be put back or tossed away like so much garbage, you held on and wiped way my tears and made me truly believe that everything was going to be ok, and that it would all work out in the end.

You have been with me through so much of my transition into the person that I am today, have always supported everything I've ever done, every hair brained business plan, every crazy thing I ever wanted to do, and you always just smiled and said ok dear. I love that you moved to the country for me. I love that you picked a house with a pool over a pole barn because it was what I wanted (even though I hardly ever go in the pool). I love that we share our home with our crazy cats. I love that you built our rescue ducks a home and pen out of cedar because it was better for them (even if it wasn't so great on our pocketbook).

I love the way you look at me and I love to look into your eyes. You're the most inspiring and amazing person I've ever had the pleasure of knowing. I've loved spending the last 18 years of our life together and I'm looking forward to one day sailing around the world with you and finally being able to support you in doing what you love because you've always supported me.

Thank you for always being there for me, for always supporting me, for always telling me how much you love me, and for just putting up with me. I know I'm not an easy person to love and I'm sure I've had you on the verge of insanity a couple of times, but you managed to make it through, and you still put up with me. Every day I thank the universe for the blessing of you, so thank you from the bottom of my heart for everything you've done for and with me. Words will never be able to adequately explain just how much you mean to me. I love you so much.

Introduction

The idea for this book was sparked by a video I saw years ago by Jim Carrey, actor and comedian. In the video, he was talking about the meaning of life and what he thought the purpose of life was. He said, "The purpose of life is to love yourself." And this struck a very deep chord with me. So deep that I immediately recognized that I did not love myself. Not very much anyway. I decided there and then to make a change to try and do what I could to love myself better, and this book is the culmination of all the years and all of the things I have done and still do, to continue to evolve into the person I was meant to be.

At the time I heard this message, I was already more than ten years deep into a journey of self-transformation. There was something so powerful and compelling in that very succinct message. *The purpose of life is to love yourself.* While I had been really working at transforming my body with exercise and diet and I was adept at meditation, I realized in those words that I did not truly love myself.

My early life was very chaotic, and I met with violence and assault. Because of the violence, I lived a good portion of my formative life in fear. Because of the fear, I became a neurotic people pleaser, and a classic Type A personality. My childhood graduated to adolescence, and then adulthood and unfortunately because of circumstances beyond my control (at least I thought) I became an alcoholic. By the time I was old enough to drink, I was a full-fledged alcoholic.

Because of things that happened earlier in my life, I did a lot of things I'm not proud of. I dated a lot of horrible men, some of them (let's be honest, most of them) were older than me and I only dated them for the fact that they supplied me with booze. I also ended up becoming a stripper, and then even worse, an adult sex worker.

I tried very hard to pretend that I had a great life, but I hated everything about it. I hated myself, I hated my family, I hated the education system, I was lonely, and I was scared, and so I drank. I drank to ease the misery. I drank because Michelob Light and Jack Daniel's were my friends, I drank to forget, and worst of all, I drank so that I could sleep at night.

I was a very high functioning alcoholic and I was very good at keeping secrets. The interesting thing is that none of my friends, or even the family I still talked to, knew that while I worked a "normal" job during the day, that at night I would go on "dates" with men for money.

You might be thinking of Pretty Woman, and while this all sounds fascinating and interesting, I can tell you that the sordid world of a sex worker is anything but interesting and it is most certainly not glamorous. It's mostly horrifying, shameful and downright dangerous.

It was during this period of my life that I started dating a guy. He was a really nice guy. Like seriously nice. He wasn't a "John", he worked with me at my legitimate day job, and he had no idea what I was doing at night. I assumed he would be like all the other men I had dated to that point. He would use me, get what he wanted, realize I was damaged goods and then move on to greener pastures.

Interesting enough though, all the men I dated, I also used them. I used them to fill a void in my life that I wasn't sure I could fill. I was clingy and neurotic and worked subconsciously to destroy every relationship. I didn't really have great relationship role models growing up, so I had no idea what a good functioning relationship should look like.

So here we are, me and my guy going out on dates and having fun and somewhere along the way, I realize that I'm really falling for him. I think he really likes me, but deep inside I'm terrified. Terrified of what he'll think when he finds the "real" me deep down inside that I've been hiding from the world.

I don't know how it happened, but he did find out about my "secret" life and the most amazing thing happened. Instead of walking away (like most people would), he tried to help me. In that moment of his absolute understanding and acceptance, I realized what he was truly giving me was unconditional love.

It was at that moment that I realized that I was capable of *being* loved. I realized that one of the holes I was trying desperately to fill was love, but it was something outside of myself. I was still to learn the lesson that Jim imparted that day, but this was the very first step in the right direction. Knowing that I was capable of being loved. In that moment of my life, he made me feel important, he made me feel like I mattered, and he made me feel like I wanted to change my life for the better. He gave me one thing I had been missing in my life until then, hope. Hope that there was something better out there in the world and that I could be a part of it. I quit drinking cold turkey!

I am happy to say that no matter how hard I worked to push him away, my guy grabbed me and pulled me closer and to this day we remain inseparable. For the longest time though, I still harbored secret fears and doubts. Fears that I wasn't good enough for him and that one day he would wake up and realize he had made a mistake and that there was someone better for him out there.

I know this is ridiculous, but this is how the mind keeps you trapped. You run on this hamster wheel of never-ending negativity and it's absolutely draining. I waited and waited and waited for the "shoe" to drop. The day he would come home and tell me he had enough of my neuroses and not being good enough and that he was leaving, or worse, telling me to get my stuff and get out (which is how a previous relationship ended).

Here I was again, searching for something outside of myself. Living in fear that who I was depended on what he thought of me or how his feelings of me justified my existence and my way of life.

I still didn't realize that I was really missing

something in my life, or if I did realize something was missing, I didn't know what it was until that fateful day when I happened on that video of Jim Carrey. It was then that I realized that I truly didn't love myself and was just trying to make myself the best "version" I wanted the public, and even my husband, to see. I still had this "secret" inner life that was all turmoil.

Once I heard that one clear message, that was all I needed to hear for all the puzzle pieces of my life to fit together. For the proverbial light bulb to click on and for me to say "Ah-Ha" that's what it's been all along!

Now that I knew what I was missing, it became my mission to learn to love myself. In learning to love myself, my life has transformed to new levels of joy, abundance, and peace that it's truly remarkable. It is this place of being that I want to bring you to, dear reader, and within these pages, I hope that you can find that *one* "ah-ha" that will help you to truly ascend to the best version of yourself that you were born to be. You truly are a magnificent, beautiful and divine being and my hope is that I can help you to see and truly believe that.

Brightest Blessings,
Crystal Castle

Section One

NOURISHING MIND REALIZING YOUR TRUE POTENTIAL

Chapter 1
EDUCATION

I have a magnet that is on one of my filing cabinets that says, "When your education is finished, so are you". I don't know who said that, but it's something I have always taken to heart. Education is something you should continually strive for. Learning new things not only occupies your time (in a constructive fashion), it also helps to keep your brain young by continuing to create new neural pathways.

Learning new things is also a great way to keep your life interesting. You can never know too much I always say, and by learning more you become empowered to do so much more with your life. Education and learning don't have to mean taking a class or formal education but learning something you previously didn't know. Do you know the history of the town where you live? How about the meaning of your favorite song? Do you know why the sky is blue? Spending time learning more about the world we live in is a great way to become more connected. Not only to yourself but to those around you.

People think I'm crazy because I'm actively enrolled in five different colleges. I'm always looking at continuing education classes and the community center classes to see if there is anything interesting that I think I might like to learn about. I recently took a class on writing a book in 60 days. I learned a lot and am glad I took that class (it was through a community center, was one evening for about 2.5 hours and cost around $30). There are plenty of places where you can learn a lot of stuff, stuff you didn't even know you needed to learn.

The internet is also an amazing resource. I have a friend whose wife is a high school math teacher. Now when I was in school, I had a tutor to help me with math, but she just has the children go onto YouTube to learn how to do the problems that they can't figure out. They can do it at home and for free. Where the heck was YouTube when I was a kid? You can literally learn how to take a car apart and put it back together again on YouTube.

I recently used an instructional video on YouTube to learn how to make glitter jars, they are beautiful and amazing to watch, I highly recommend making one. I made a bunch of Christmas gifts last year and gave them to all my friends. They all LOVED them. Great ideas and things to learn are all available at the click of the mouse and the push of a few buttons on the internet.

Action Step: Try to think of things that you have always wanted to learn about that you just never did. Make a list of five things you have always wanted to maybe take a class on or watch an instructional video on. Once you have that list of five things completed, start looking for ways to learn what it is you want to learn.

Some wonderful things to try and learn are DIY household cleaners, homemade gifts (like the glitter jars that I did), decorating ideas for the holidays, how-to's, cooking (I recently watched a series of instructional videos from Hay House author Donna Schwenk on making cultured foods), exercise (another great series I watched was from Hay House done by Jillian Michaels on exercise). There really is no end to the number of things that you can learn online.

I myself have put together a series of instructional videos that you can access free on connecting to self and source. You can find these videos at www. mindfulshift.org/bookbonuses. These videos are an amazing tool for you to spend time learning from and putting the tips and tricks to use in the future.

Chapter 2
READING

I know this one may be a sticking point for some people because not everyone enjoys reading. To be honest, that statement really makes me sad. Sad because I feel that those who don't enjoy reading don't really understand what they are missing out on. Reading transforms. Not only does it transform you, but it also transports you to new and wondrous places.

When I was a child, I would read any book I could get my hands on. It didn't matter what the subject, if it was a book, I read it. I had a teacher once tell me that I didn't just read books, I devoured them. I read fiction and non-fiction, biographies and always carried with me my sturdy dictionary. I had that dictionary so that I could look up the meanings of words that I didn't know and also figure out how to pronounce them, because, let's be honest, who in their right mind really knows how to pronounce hours d'oeuvres the first time they encounter it (unless you're French or Canadian, of course)? I'm also the dork that read the entire Encyclopedia Britannica. Just because.

I bring up reading because reading is important. It is a vital tool to help you tap into your true potential. Not only is it an untapped resource of infinite potential, you will learn more than you ever thought possible.

Now, when it comes to reading, you don't have to read novels. Heavens no, there are so many different things to be read, magazines, periodicals, blogs, online resources, comics, directions (did I say directions? Yes, you should always read the directions.)

You can infer that you have an idea on how to do something, and then read the instructions to prove you were right to begin with, a win-win if you ask me!

Action Step: If possible (if it's your thing), come up with a list of books you would like to read. It can be short or long, doesn't matter as long as you make a list. You can check out different periodicals from the library to see whether you might want to subscribe, or better yet, join a subscription program like Amazon, Google, or Scribd to try lots of different material for a small fee. You can also download my list of 10 books everybody should read from www. mindfulshift.org/bookbonuses.

Chapter 3
CHALLENGES

*I*f you don't challenge yourself, you will never realize what you can become.

What is a challenge, except something that gets you out of your comfort zone and into a space that will help you grow and develop as a person? A challenge is a wonderful way to expand your horizons and to try something you may never have previously thought of doing. It's also a way to learn new things or maybe learn a different way to do something you already know or to expand on current knowledge to see if you can learn something you didn't already know.

You can also see challenges as opportunities. You can't stay in your comfort zone and keep learning. A lot of people are afraid to challenge themselves because of fear of failure. Instead of seeing an opportunity, we focus on what it will be like to fail. By avoiding challenges, we don't have the opportunity to learn, particularly about ourselves. The interesting thing about your comfort zone is that once you move past the dividing line, your comfort zone changes, it will never go back to the way it was before.

Challenges shape who we are, make us more well-rounded, teach us lessons, help us learn and grow and be stronger. Fear kills more dreams than failure ever could.

I use challenges to move me out of my comfort zone all the time. One way I do that is through public speaking. Everyone asks me all the time how I do it. They lament that they could never get up in front of a group of people and talk, one woman said she would faint, another said she would die. I told them, it is tough and certainly terrifying, but I don't let that stop me. I sometimes feel light-headed, sometimes I feel like I want to throw up and then run away crying, but I swallow hard, take a deep breath and just start talking.

The funny thing about public speaking is that if you're talking about something that you are truly passionate about, the time does pass quickly. I just speak like I'm talking to a friend and it makes it so much easier. Usually, I have a small habit of running over on time because I am so very passionate about what I teach that sometimes it's hard to convey everything that I need to in such a small amount of time.

Another possibility would be to challenge yourself to stop a bad habit. I gave myself one such challenge not that long ago, to stop cracking my knuckles, and while it was very difficult to remember to stay present and not mindfully keep repeating the same behavior, with practice I was able to stop.

Action Step: Figure a small thing you could do each day to help move you out of your comfort zone. Challenge yourself to try something different, to drive a new way to work, to sleep on the other side of the bed, use a different toothpaste, start recycling. These are all small things that don't require a large amount of energy, but surprisingly enough make a difference when you make a conscious effort to switch a daily habit for something different. You will realize just how automatic your normal routines are, and if you're a game person, you will find it fun to try and challenge yourself to do something different.

Chapter 4
LEARNING NEW SKILLS

This one to me, is *the* most fun, because I truly love to learn new things. Beginning every November and into December, I start putting together a mastery list for the new year. I quit doing resolutions years ago and started doing mastery lists. On that list is always a new skill I want to learn. I've learned a lot of skills over the years. Some I love (Master Gardener) and some not so much (metalsmithing for jewelry making) but I always have at least one skill and sometimes two on my list.

Learning a new skill really gets your brain grooving. And what I mean by grooving is you're creating new neural pathways in the brain when you learn a new skill. It's like riding a bike. It takes a while to get it, but once you do, you can have not ridden a bike in 20 years and get on one and it's like no time has passed. Muscle memory due to the neural pathway created when acquiring the skill.

It's important to try to learn new things (or expand on your current knowledge) to keep the pathways clear of cobwebs and to help create new pathways to keep your brain fresh and young. Learning new skills helps with memory and makes your brain more responsive. Adult learning is great for your health and has research has shown to slow the onset of dementia and Alzheimer's (1).

The interesting thing is that your brain is like a muscle. Just like muscles, the more you use them, the stronger they grow, so by using your brain more to learn a new skill, you're helping to make your brain grow stronger.

Action Step: Try to think of things that you have always wanted to try, do, or learn that you just haven't gotten around to. Don't think about how impossible some things may be, or how you'll find the time, just make the list. Ever wanted to learn the piano? Who cares if you don't own a piano, just put it on the list. Once you have a list of at least ten items, work on doing them one at a time. Start small and work your way up. Always wanted to try karate? Find a class and give it a shot (a lot of places will let you try free the first time).

I try to make it a habit to learn one new skill a year so that isn't too terribly daunting. Some you will love, like the last skill I learned (as of the writing of this book), which was sailing (I took a 4-day ASA 101 & 103 sailing course - OUTSTANDING). Some you might not enjoy so much – like when I took my metalsmithing for jewelry course. It turns out I don't really care for it, but I did learn how much work goes into the crafting of handmade jewelry, so now I have a greater appreciation for handcrafted items and the prices that crafters put on them. I can also now look at something and tell if it was machine or hand made, so I really learned a lot. Next up on my list of skills…Photoshop. You may not like what you learn, but the key is to at least try something new and see where it takes you.

Chapter 5
GAMES

*G*ames are a great way to learn new skills, brush up on old skills and build great neural pathways, keeping the brain healthier. Games of skill like chess, poker, bridge, backgammon and Mahjong or games of strategy like Risk®, Stratego®, Civilization®, Chess, Monopoly®, Scrabble®, Diplomacy®, and backgammon. These kinds of games make you think and make you anticipate then plan and prepare based on what could happen in the future.

These types of games are great for your health as they help you to focus more on the task at hand and possible future outcomes than worrying about what is going on in the world. An added benefit, the more you play the better you get. Better at anticipating moves, thinking fast on your feet.

"Success is where preparation and opportunity meet" - Bobby Unsher

You gain better observation skills, a deeper consideration of options, greater agility, more flexibility, improved decision making. Plus, it has the added benefit of creating a community with others since most strategy games aren't played alone. You get a good bonding experience with your peers and it creates a sense of purpose and belonging when you're with a group of likeminded people attempting to achieve the same goal. Even if that goal is to beat you.

If you don't know anyone close to you who would be interested in playing games with you, try Meetup.com. There are always local Meetups near your area with people that have similar interests. Even if the group is a group that is far more skilled than you are, they are almost always willing to teach new people the ropes. It's a great way to meet new people too.

Action Step: Find a simple strategy game and try playing. Try to incorporate them occasionally into your routine. If you can, try for some regular consistency, like once a month. For a date night, my husband and I played Battleship® (yeah, you sunk my Battleship®) and it was easily one of the best date nights ever (we built a fort too!).

Chapter 6
ENRICHMENT

To me, enrichment means finding something (or things) that add pure value to your life. Or, in turn, recognizing all the things that you already have that add value to your life that you either don't recognize (see) or that you take for granted.

Take, for example, relationships. The people in your life either give value or take value away from your life. It's up to you to see the value each person brings (be it positive or negative) to you. My mom always said "Crystal, a person in your life is always someone you can learn and lesson from. Even the bad people, they are examples of how not to live your life." My mom was always full of what I call my life's little lessons. There is so much in the world to give more meaning to your life.

It's possible that you believe that there is no good in the world, or nothing that really adds meaning and I'll tell you what Dr. Wayne Dyer says, "When you change the way you look at things, the things you look at change." This has a very profound meaning to me because if you expect the world to be negative, dark, and dreary, rarely will you ever be disappointed.

The word exists exactly how you expect it to be.

In order to have a more fulfilling life, you need to find things that can enrich your life. You need to be able to see the good in things and the positive in any situation. You can do this by making sure that you have a positive attitude and being happy in the face of adversity. Sometimes this sounds like an insurmountable task, particularly when you have serious issues to content. These situations are far from ideal, but there is a reason you are experiencing them. By trying to see the good that will come from the situation, or the lesson to be learned you will help to improve your outlook on life and be happier.

In that same regard, you need to surround yourself with good people. You are the average sum of the people you surround yourself with. If you surround yourself with negative people, you will have a negative outlook. If you surround yourself with happy, positive people, your outlook will be better, and you will be happier for it.

<u>Action Step:</u> Get some paper and a pen or pencil and write down a list of things that add value or meaning to your life. If you can't think of twenty right off the bat, no worries. Just write twenty numbers and leave the list where you can see it daily as a reminder to be on the lookout.

As you see the list daily, you are training your subconscious mind to be or the lookout for those things which meet the criteria. Don't be surprised if one day the flood gates open and suddenly you keep coming up with more and more things to add to the list.

Once you reach twenty, you should start a daily journal to get down all of the things you appreciate that add value and maybe even add some items you have been meaning to get to like volunteering or spending time with friends and family and then start making plans to do those things more often!

Chapter 7
DAYDREAMING & VISUALIZATION

"There is no agony like bearing an untold story inside you." – Zora Neale

Daydreaming is something that important to your very being. Everything you are and everything you do comes from thought, from your imagination. It's important to spend time imagining and visualizing exactly what you want, where you want your life to go and any goals you might be trying to achieve. By doing this, you're training your brain to recognize subtle and seemingly insignificant things as being relevant to your life and your goals. They became a part of your unconscious awareness and help to see potential in every situation.

Daydreaming and visualization are ways for you to see possibilities. Even things that you think may be unattainable, thinking of them being them into the realm of possibility and your brain will constantly seek ways to make that possibility a reality sooner than you ever thought possible. Daydreaming or visualizing about goals and things you would like to accomplish is a great way to help bring them to you faster.

Every time you think of something, you're asking your subconscious mind to become aware and soon avenues or pathways to your goal start to just magically show up. These are called synchronicities, but it is just your subconscious mind bringing out of the thousands of things that things it sees daily into your conscious awareness. Then, it's up to you to make the decision to either walk toward or away from whatever it was you were seeking.

Daydreaming and visualization also have additional health benefits. Using your imagination will help you tap into creativity and help with problem-solving. It can help you be more empathetic and can help you to calm down and enter a meditative state reducing stress and blood pressure.

Action Step: Think of one goal that you're trying to accomplish right now. Spend some time (five minutes or so) every day just daydreaming about what your life will be like when you reach that goal. How will it make you feel? How will you act? Then spend some time trying to think of ways that you can accomplish that goal faster.

Do you know someone who could help you? Do you have ideas on how you could get to where you need to be but don't have any way to really act on those ideas? Don't think of the things that aren't possible, keep impossibility out of the equation and just dream about all the great things you could do when you accomplish your goal. Then just start paying attention. You will be amazed at how quickly things, opportunities, and people will start showing up to help lead you toward your goal.

A great resource for trying small experiments is reading Pam Grout's book E^2. It is amazing (and kind of creepy) how well those small energy experiments work in that book.

Chapter 8
BE TRUE TO YOURSELF

"Be yourself, no matter what they say." - Sting

*B*eing true to yourself is about being *You*. The funny thing is most people don't know who "they" are. Sure, you're mom, daughter, spouse, sister, friend, employee, boss, co-worker. But when you're not wearing those hats, who are you really? Down to your very core, who were you meant to be? You weren't born to wear hats; you were born to be (state your name out loud). For most of my life, I lived by everyone else rules and expectations of me. I conformed to the norm's society placed on me due to those hats, and the rest of me got lost in the shuffle. Somewhere along the way, I found myself again and I have not let that real me go.

Once I learned who the real me was, I began to see how I was meant to live my life and to value myself as an individual and for my uniqueness. I think that if we're trying to be what our peers, family, and society wants us to be we don't value ourselves, because we know, deep down, that we aren't being authentic. That by being fake, were not truly valuable. Once we recognize our own individuality and our unique presence, then and only then, can we truly see the value of who we really are and love ourselves for it.

"Why fit in, when you were born
to stand out!" – Dr. Seuss

<u>Action Step:</u> This might be an interesting one for you to try and do. Grab some paper and something to write with. Set a timer for three minutes and during those three minutes, write down all the hats that you wear on a daily, weekly and monthly basis. This could be any one of the items listed above and anything additional like a cleaner, gardener, launderer, etc.

After you have your list, put them in numerical order from highest priority to lowest priority. Then next to each item write whether you like wearing that hat or not. Some hats we wear because we must, not because we want to.

Now get another page ready. Set a timer for another three minutes and during that time, write down all the things you dream of doing, or things that you enjoy doing like artist, musician, designer, punk rocker, etc. These are going to be the things that you are going to aspire to that society generally would frown upon. Something like being a bodybuilder. If you're in your 60's, 70's or 80's, this might be something that is not highly acceptable by society's standards, because the majority of people don't understand that someone older is even capable of doing something like that.

Once you come up with the list of things you dream of aspiring to, start writing a list of the things that are keeping you from achieving those ideals of yourself that you aspire to. Once you have that list you should keep it where you can see it on a regular basis and every time you look at it, think about the reasons why you *should* do those things instead of the reasons why you shouldn't. Use the list of reasons why you can't as the motivation to move out of your comfort zone to move toward your truth and your true potential. You were put here for a reason and that reason was to be happy and to love yourself. If you are doing things for other people and not for yourself, you will never truly be happy. You need to look past those people to the other side of the fear and just make that jump. As terrifying as it might seem, you will be far more miserable if you stay stuck where you are as opposed to disappointing a few people. You are responsible for yourself and your own happiness just as everyone else is responsible for their own happiness. You can't make anyone else happy; you can only make yourself happy, and you never will be if you aren't living your most authentic life.

Chapter 9
EXPAND YOUR HORIZONS

There is an amazingly beautiful world just outside of our doors. We live in the most amazing world with so many fascinating cultures and people, yet it seems that quite a few of us have never spent time learning about, exploring or experiencing all these wonderful people and places.

A lot of us never travel outside of our hometown, let alone our home state or even out of the country. Some of this is because of a lack of funds to travel, but mostly it's being in your comfort zone. You've only known this area, this specific part of town and you're afraid to venture farther outside of the areas that you know to experience the unknown because it's foreign and unfamiliar.

I remember when I first moved to the city of

Detroit. For those of you who don't know, Detroit is a very large city (almost 143 square miles). It is also a confusing city because it was designed on a hub-and-spoke configuration as opposed to a more traditional grid plan, which means the streets run on diagonals instead of straight lines. This can be extremely confusing when trying to get around. Whenever I went anywhere, I ended up staying on just the main roads that I knew because I didn't want to get lost.

I was always confused though, as to why some of the roads that I was on, how they would hit other roads twice. Say for example you have a road like Grand Boulevard (which is the road I lived on in Detroit when I was going to college). It was split into East Grand Boulevard and West Grand Boulevard (where I lived) and the split happened at what's known as Mid-Town Detroit. But this road hit a straight freeway (I-94) in two different places. I couldn't understand why it did that (or how). One day I pulled out a map and realized that some of the roads were designed almost like half circles. It went from the Detroit river on one side and then it went in a half-circle around Detroit and back to the Detroit river on the other side of downtown. It was also while I was looking at the map that I could see some of the major roads I was familiar with intersecting through a lot of the major metropolitan areas.

I realized while looking at that map that it didn't matter where I was in Detroit, because of the way the city was set up, if I was on a road and just kept driving, eventually I would come to a road that I knew and could easily find my way back home. So, I decided to start taking different ways to and from work and school. Every day I would pick a different road and just drive. It was an eye-opening adventure for me. I saw some wonderful neighborhoods, found some amazing stores and restaurants that I previously didn't know about and now I'm no longer afraid to drive around in downtown Detroit because it's all very familiar. If ever given the opportunity, I highly recommend a trip to our beautiful downtown area. Over the years it's gotten a very bad rap, but it's coming along very nicely and it's an amazing city to visit.

I also remember how wonderful it was to visit another country for the first time. Now, living in Michigan right next to Canada, I've been to another country many times, but since Canada is like visiting a neighboring state to us, it really doesn't seem like it's that big of a deal. My first other country experience was traveling to Ireland to visit some friends and family. That was a real eye-opening experience. It was amazing to me to see how people live in a completely different frame of mind and mentality than we do in the United States. It was fun to spend time learning about some of their history and culture and even a little Gaelic.

Action Step: Think of someone whom you are acquainted with (or a friend of a friend if you don't know anyone you can think of) that is from a different culture or background than yours. Ask that person out for a meal or coffee. See how you can both spend time getting to know one another better and learning about each other's cultures. If you want to be really daring, try going to another country and fully immersing yourself in the culture learning about the history, eating the foods and enjoying yourself.

Chapter 10
BE COMPASSIONATE

*B*eing compassionate to others is an admirable quality to cultivate. Compassion for others means that you can see and understand where someone has come from and then you can also understand what they have been through and that you don't judge them. It is important to not feel pity or sorry for them, but to truly "get" them and the struggles they have been through to get to where they are now.

True compassion is the practice of cultivating love for oneself. Once we care capable of truly loving ourselves, then we will be capable of loving and understanding others. To truly love ourselves, we must accept ourselves for who we are, where we are, regardless of what we may have done in our lives. This book is the culmination of the years that I have spent learning to truly love myself, and honestly, until that moment when I heard Jim Carrey's speech, I didn't realize that I never truly learned to love, accept or appreciate myself. I still harbored deep resentments for things that had happened to me in the past that made me really dislike myself and even worse, I hated myself for all the things that I had done that were what I considered to be the wrong choices.

I have made some seriously bad career mistakes, some even worse relationship mistakes, and there is so much that I could have done better in my life that I was always beating myself up for the things I should have done differently. It even creeps in now in my life. I do something and my mind says, "You Big Dummy - in my grandfather's voice because he was always saying that - I can't believe you DID/SAID that". There is nothing that you can do to get away from those negative thoughts. All you can do is accept that they are there and will always be there trying to keep you small, while you're really meant to play big.

We're all like this, we all have these negative thoughts that run through our heads on a constant negative feedback loop. But it doesn't have to affect you. By accepting that those things are done and that nothing can change them, then you begin to start the healing process. Once you accept and then begin to love those parts of you, those terribly faulted parts of you, then you will really have true love and compassion for yourself. It's ok to be sad on occasion for things in the past, but it's important not to dwell on them.

Treat yourself like you would a wounded child. If you saw a wounded child, would you kick it some more? I would certainly hope that you wouldn't, but you need to see yourself sometimes like that wounded child and be kind, gentle, loving and compassionate. You wouldn't look at that child and say, what did you do to become wounded? Did you deserve it? You would wrap your arms around that child with love and try as hard as you could to protect it. This is what you need to do to your inner self, wrap your arms around yourself and do what you can to protect yourself, including protecting yourself from your negative self-talk,

We all do what we need to in order to survive and we all do the best that we can with the knowledge we have at the time to make the best choices for ourselves. Sometimes it's the best we can do, and we must be ok with that. Of course, as we grow older and wiser, we realize that sometimes we made some terrible mistakes, but that was in the past and that is over and done with now. All you can do is learn to let go of those mistakes, love yourself regardless of them and move on and be kinder to yourself in the future.

Action Step: Find one small thing from your past that you hold against yourself. We're good at harboring resentments so it shouldn't be too difficult. Once you have that one small thing, spend some time thinking about the situation as you remember it. Once you have done that, take a piece of paper and a writing utensil and then write your inner child a letter. Tell your inner child that you're sorry for all the times you were unable to protect him/her/they/them and that you really wanted to, but you were unable to at that time. Tell your inner child how much that situation hurt you and is still hurting you to this day because you think about it often, and then tell your inner child that you love them and that you will do whatever you can to protect them in the future. Tell them that you forgive yourself for being unable to do anything at the time, and that even though you wish the situation was different, or that the outcome was different that you love yourself regardless of your decision at the time. This task might seem like a hard one to accomplish, but it's one of the most important out of all the action steps within this book. This one lesson will be the best one you can learn because it's from this healing that your life will begin to fall into place, and you will be happier for it.

Section Two

NOURISHING BODY BUILDING YOUR TRUE POTENTIAL

Chapter 11
EXERCISE AND MOVEMENT

We weren't created to be sedentary beings, yet according to the British Journal for Sports Medicine, the average person sits for eight to ten hours per day (Buckley, et al., 2015). Our physiology is such that in order to thrive, we must continuously move. As we age and get busier in our lives, we find ourselves sitting more and more. Sit in the car on the way to work. Sit at the desk for 8-9 hours. Sit in the car on the way home. Sit at the table (hopefully) for dinner then sit in front of a TV or computer and while away the rest of our hours until it's time to go to sleep.

We need to move in order to maintain a healthy body. The problem of being sedentary has gotten so bad that the scientific community has coined the term "Sitting Disease" to describe many of the health problems associated with an overly sedentary lifestyle. One of the biggest problems with sitting so much is that it causes our tendons to become shorter and far less flexible. Rigid almost. This causes problems with flexibility and can cause significant pain and hamper movement. Our bodies are the only homes we will ever live in for our entire lives, therefore we need to do everything that we can to maintain that home to the best of our abilities. I'm not saying that you need to go out now and join a gym and start a crazy workout routine, but some form of daily movement is essential for wellbeing.

Let's put it this way, if you were given the choice of a car which would you choose, a well-cared-for and maintained Lamborghini, or a beat down, rusted out piece of junk that looks like it's on its last leg? I know which one I would choose, the Lamborghini for sure. I can say this because I used to be that beat down, rusted out piece of junk and I was literally on my last leg.

I was oblivious to the fact that I was running myself into the ground abusing my body with food, alcohol, tobacco, and lack of exercise. To make matters worse, I used to rely heavily on medication to help get me through the day because I had asthma and I was diagnosed with acute hypertension and high cholesterol. Get that I said "had". Yes, that's right, <u>had</u>. I was given an ultimatum by a health care professional, make a change or meet my maker. I made the decision to make a change and change I did. I went from being overweight, out of shape, and on daily meds to becoming a sponsored triathlete in a matter of a few years and then transitioned into ultra-running (no more meds either!).

The point of this story here is that I fixed my broke down piece of junk and turned it into the well cared for Lamborghini and I know now that as I care for and maintain my body, it will last me longer than it had as the broken down piece of junk. I decided that my body was to become my temple and adjusted what I did to myself, and the results were amazing. I'm literally typing this while on a plane back from the most amazing hiking trip with my husband. We hiked over 20 miles in a few days in a few different mountain ranges in Washington state, and if I wasn't in the best shape of my life because of the care I decided to take, I wouldn't have been able to do that. We accumulated over 13,000 feet of elevation on this trip as well as the distance, so I'm here to tell you that anything is possible. If you had told me that I would be climbing mountains 10 years ago I would have laughed at you and then wheezed because all of my laughs turned into coughing fits where I couldn't get air, yet I just climbed to 10,000 feet above sea level without the use of medication because I made the decision to change my life.

Action Step: Start with something small and start doing some sort of daily movements. I started with short walks and then transitioned into walking/running/walking. I'm not saying you need to go out tomorrow and run a marathon (most people don't like running and to be honest, I don't blame you; I only ran to prove to myself that I could), just move. Go outside every day and do a quick 10-minute walk. Don't really feel like it? Get a dog and then take it for walks. Better yet, borrow one from a friend or neighbor, and then you'll make a new friend, and both will be excited to get out and get moving (hopefully, at least).

Check out meetup.com or myfitnesspal.com to see if there are any walking or fitness groups near to you to join. Those are always fun because you get to meet new people and then you can talk and walk at the same time, plus if you have an accountability partner, that will help to motivate you more to continue with your daily movement. If you do nothing else in the book, at the very least maintain some form of daily movement *outside* of your normal daily routine.

If you walk a lot for your job (or stand, etc.) you

do the same thing over and over and there is a point where it no longer becomes exercise, you plateau and it's just your normal everyday life so make sure to do something beyond what you normally do daily. You can also access some wonderful exercises I have put together for you here at www.mindfulshift. com/bookbonuses. I have made these exercises easy, simple, and fun. They will give you the much-needed movement necessary to keep yourself in top physical form.

If you already do daily exercises, awesome for you and keep up the great work. *Your* task will be to encourage someone that you know who could use the extra movement, and we all know someone who could use the extra encouragement, to join you in whatever task that you do. To encourage and motivate someone else to move is a monumental feat and you should work to get someone else to where you are. It will make you feel so much better.

Chapter 12
PROPER NUTRITION

With our fast-paced and hectic life, it can be easy to overlook something as vitally important as nutrition. We rush here and there, and when we think to eat; we do what most people do. We open a package and put something in the microwave or drive through a fast-food restaurant to eat. Well, what is that thing that they are trying to feed you? It says chicken on the menu, but that doesn't look like chicken!

Anyway, we give very little thought to what we're eating, when, why, or how. If we're celebrating, we eat. If we're happy, we eat. If we're sad, we eat. If we're tired, we eat. If we're bored, guess what we do? We eat. We eat mindlessly with little regard to what we're eating, why we're eating it, or exactly how much we're consuming. We use food to keep us company, provide us comfort, keep us occupied and calm us down, but that's not what food is meant for.

Because we're so busy all the time, we eat poorly and run ourselves into the ground and we wonder why we're so sick. Spending more time nourishing our bodies with the delicious, and fresh food that we need in order to survive and be healthy is really what it's all about. Taking the time to find out is we have vitamin and mineral deficiencies in our bodies and then taking the necessary steps to help replace them with fruits and vegetables.

When eating, doing so mindfully, pay attention to the food, give thanks to the food for providing sustenance for you and remember to give thanks to the universe for providing us with delicious nourishment. Make sure you're paying attention to the quantities you're eating as well and don't just eat because you are bored or angry or upset. Think about your feelings and eat only when you're truly hungry.

When are you actually hungry? Not as often as you would think, it turns out. Ask yourself when you start to feel hungry, am I really hungry? If your body says yes, then drink a glass of water and then wait 10-15 minutes and ask the same thing again. If the answer is still yes, then get yourself something to eat, but get yourself a specific amount of food and don't go over. Practice what the Japanese call Hara hachi bun me, which means to only eat until you are about 80% full. Can you even tell when you're 80% full? If you begin to practice Hara hachi bun me, you won't be likely to overeat, and you won't feel so overstuffed that you feel uncomfortable and your food will digest better. It's also an easy way for you to be more mindful of your food intake. If you're paying attention to how much you're eating, you won't be able to focus on anything else and then you will become a mindful eating master.

The quality of the food that you eat is important too. Eating good quality, as organic as possible, food becomes beneficial for you. Our systems are so bombarded with toxins and harmful bacteria that it's sometimes overwhelming for our bodies to be able to process. This is sometimes why we have things like complete system breakdowns in things like IBS, Chron's Disease, Auto-Immune Disorders all the way up to cancer.

Our body has so much difficulty battling all of the things it comes in contact with on a daily basis, and then to top it off, you add to the pile by eating lots of meat (which is very hard on the digestive system), dairy, wheat and sugar (which are the largest causes of the inflammatory response in your body) and most of those items are conventionally grown, which means the use of pesticides and herbicides is standard practice. It's a toxic, meltdown mess that can wreak havoc on your digestive tract (the source of your immune system) and in turn lead to system breakdowns causing disease.

Eating lots of fruits and vegetables that are high in fiber, reducing the amount of meat, dairy, gluten and eliminating added sugar will help your body be on the road to recovery and you will see, and feel, the difference in a short time.

Action Step: When you first wake up in the morning, drink a warm glass (8 - 12oz) of water with lemon juice (preferably freshly squeezed). This practice helps you to start your digestive tract off in the right direction. It will help to boost immunity and your metabolism prior to eating anything. You can be brave and add a pinch of cayenne if you want to, but I don't prefer this myself as I don't like peppery tastes.

Begin to attempt the Hara hachi bun me practice. See if you can make a game of it, to try and gauge when you're truly 80% full. That is generally the point of satiation, but your stomach doesn't communicate that quickly with your brain so, by the time you realize your stomach is full, it's usually too late. Engaging in mindful eating practices will help you to lose weight, sleep better and feel better.

Chapter 13
HYDRATION

We are made of 60% water and we live on a planet that is 70% water. It makes sense then that water would be the most essential part of our nutritional wellbeing. Most people eat not because they are hungry, but because they are dehydrated. It's been estimated that 75% of American adults are chronically dehydrated. Water is a fluid of life and it is essential for vital functions to be performed. It helps lubricate joints for movement, supports the movement of cells throughout the body, and aids in digestion and elimination.

Making sure you are properly hydrated takes some planning and preparation. You must make sure that you have water bottles on hand (preferably refillable) if you are going to be out and about. Make sure you start your day with a big glass of water to aid digestion and kick start your metabolism.

Avoiding dehydrating food and drinks is also key to remaining properly hydrated. Try to avoid alcohol, a high-protein diet, salty foods, sugary drinks, and coffee. Now I know you may think I'm being a barbarian by asking you to do this, but your body will surely thank you for it. I personally have one cup of coffee per day and occasionally, I'll have a soda (though I eschew all alcohol and highly recommend you do as well).

In order to determine your daily water intake needs in ounces, you can multiply your weight by 2/3. For example, if you weigh 150 pounds, you would multiply 150 x 2/3, which equals 100 ounces of water per day. If you think that you couldn't possibly drink that much water, then try drinking at least 3 glasses of water to start off with per day (12oz glasses). You can work your way up to more in the future. If you don't like the taste of plain water, try adding fruit to the water for some extra flavor and try to stay away from water flavor additives.

Action Step: Start habit of drinking a glass (8 – 12 oz.) of warm water with the juice of one lemon 15-30 minutes before your first meal of the day. Try and see if you can drink 3 to 4 12-ounce glasses of water per day. I have included some delicious recipes you can download for fruit infused water from www. mindfulshift.com/bookbonuses

Chapter 14
SKINCARE

Most people don't realize it, but your skin is the largest organ of your body. It is also your first line of defense against disease, microbes, and viruses. As the first line of defense, it's very important to take the time to properly care for your skin. What does proper skincare entail? Good skincare starts with what you eat and drink. Eating a good diet with plenty of nutritious fruits and vegetables (to provide vitamins and minerals) and plenty of water for hydration. Hydration is one of the most important things for beautiful and vibrant skin.

Almost as important as what you put into your body is what you put *on* your body. As an organ, your skin absorbs everything you put onto it and everything your skin comes into contact with, including your environment. Things like chemicals, petroleum by-products, smoke, smog and any aerosol products that your skin encounters will end up being absorbed by your skin and then the ingredients will end up in your bloodstream.

It is very imperative that you not allow any toxic chemicals on to your skin, regardless of how "safe" some companies may call a product. Your health depends on it. Using all-natural personal care products is the best way to go for beautiful and healthy skin. Things that don't contain parabens, petroleum by-products, non RSPO palm oil, plastic microbeads, phthalates, fragrance (parfum), artificial colors/dyes, triclosan, sodium laurel and sodium laureth sulfates, formaldehyde, toluene, propylene glycol, siloxanes, and PEG compounds.

A great way to take care of your skin is dry brushing. Dry brushing is the act of taking a natural bristle brush and using it to literally brush your skin. Doing this provides a host of benefits. It helps to slough off dead skin, it improves circulation and stimulates lymph function, which is important because the lymphatic system is the second circulatory system and the one responsible for immune response and helps rid the body of toxins. Dry brushing will help your skin look vibrant and smooth. Plus, dry brushing helps you to pay attention to parts of your body often neglected in your regular beauty care routine.

I learned about the importance of skincare and skincare ingredients when I was younger. I have multiple chemical sensitivities and have learned that if I use products that have a lot of chemicals, dyes or fragrance that it makes me break out in hives or the strong scents give me migraines. I learned even more when I became vegan. I was so worried about the products on the market and the ingredients they contained. The easiest thing for me to do was to start making my own products. Making my own personal care products helps on a few different levels. I can control the ingredients and I can also help to minimize waste that goes into the landfill or to recycling by making my own items. For the things that I do not make, my knowledge has helped me to become hyper vigilant in making sure that all of the items I do purchase come from good sources and contain ingredients that are good for me and good for the environment.

Action Step: Take a few minutes to look at the ingredients of all the products you use to put on your skin daily. See if there are any natural alternatives to any of the chemical-laden products you may be using. The Environmental Working Group has an online guide called the Skin-Deep database where you can search their database to see if your products carry potentially harmful or toxic ingredients. The Environmental Working Group is a third-party independent research laboratory whose mission is to empower people to live healthier lives in a healthier environment. They are a non-profit, non-partisan group dedicated to helping people understand the ingredients in the day to day products and food they use and consume. The Environmental Working Group also has a guide on the most pesticide-laden foods in the industry and their site is worth visiting.

You could also try your hand at making all-natural personal care products. You can find all sorts of recipes online and tutorials showing you how to make these items. I have been handcrafting all-natural and vegan personal care products myself since 2004. It's a fun way to spend some time and to make something that you control the ingredients of.

Chapter 15
MASSAGE

*M*ost people spend all day hunched over a keyboard and staring at a computer screen. If you're not doing that, then you're likely doing something else repetitive with little time for breaks. It's even more likely that you have a high amount of stress in your daily life. Stress from work, home, friends, family, personal and professional obligations. A lot of stress can make you tense and standing or sitting in a single position with little movement will also contribute to tension in the body. The easiest way to relieve this tension is with a massage.

Massage has been around since 2700 B.C.E. Classic massage has been around since A.D. 1776. Massage helps to increase circulation, relieve anxiety, reduce stress, improve sleep, promote relaxation, relieve pain, release tension, ease depression, lower blood pressure, improve quality of life, reduce susceptibility to injury, boost immunity and increase peace of mind. With these types of benefits, you would think that everyone would be running out to get massages every day. Massage is becoming more and more popular and medical practitioners and even insurance companies are beginning to see the benefit of massage over traditional pharmaceuticals so it's becoming increasingly popular for insurance companies to cover massage for health reasons and for medical practitioners to prescribe massage as a means for restoring health.

The different types of massage are Swedish, hot stone, aromatherapy, sports, trigger point, reflexology, shiatsu, Thai, deep tissue, prenatal, lymphatic, Ayurvedic, and craniosacral. With all the options available, it should be no problem to be able to figure out which massage might work best for you and to spend some time doing some research on which might be most beneficial for you.

Action Step: See if you can find a reputable massage therapist with good reviews near you and schedule regular massage sessions as a part of your regular self-care routine. Your massage therapist will help you to feel better and you will be healthier and happier. If a massage is currently outside of the realm of possibility for you, then try a massage chair or even a chair massage. There are a lot of places in malls that offer chair massages, which are usually shorter and less expensive than traditional massage. Try and see if you can find a foot massager and use that for a short time. You could save up some money and treat yourself to a massage as a reward instead of a large celebratory meal. Massage schools offer discounted massages and you can always find deals on massage on sites like Groupon and LivingSocial.

Chapter 16
STRETCHING

*W*e've already covered in previous chapters some of the problems from leading a mostly sedentary lifestyle, but with this brings a specific problem that can be addressed simply by stretching. The problem from a sedentary lifestyle is that muscles get tight, our posture usually isn't correct (we tend to slouch) and your tendons and ligaments can shorten from sitting for too long. This can lead to pain in your back, arms, hips and legs and potentially issues with movement.

The longer you sit, the tighter your muscles, tendons, and ligaments get and then if you strain yourself too much, you can cause them to tear, resulting in an injury that can take a long time to heal, or even require surgery. The easiest way is to remedy this problem is with regular movement or exercise, and by stretching. Have you ever watched a dancer or gymnast and wondered how in the world they can move the way that they do? The answer is regular exercise and of course, stretching. Regular stretching will help to release tension in tight muscles, lengthen and soften ligaments and tendons, and will also help joints be less stiff and sore in the long run.

Regular stretching improves posture, increases flexibility and range of motion, reduces pain, improves energy levels, promotes blood circulation, improves blood flow to muscles, is great for stress relief, and increases stability.

Action Step: Download my sitting to stretching guide and start practicing the simple, short stretches daily to help gain back your flexibility from www. mindfulshift.org/bookbonuses.

Chapter 17
YOGA

*Y*oga is an amazing tool to help build a strong foundation for your body with a practice that will help to unite mind, body, and spirit through poses or 'asanas', focused breathing or 'pranayama', and meditation. Not only will yoga help unite mind, body, and spirit, it will also help with the issues discussed in the previous chapter (stiff and tight muscles, tendons and ligaments) by helping to stretch all your joints, you also improve circulation, cardiovascular health, posture, strength, and breathing.

By performing yoga poses correctly and regularly, you will improve many areas in your life. Regular yoga practice can help you sleep better, help you digest food better, relax and unwind after a stressful day/week, improve your health, increase strength, improve balance, increased wellbeing, decreased joint pain, and you will generally meet amazing people who can brighten your sphere of influence. Yoga is a great all-around exercise to help you focus, become more disciplined, be healthier and feel better in general.

<u>Action Step:</u> See if you can find a yoga class nearby to try out for a week to see if you enjoy it. Most yoga classes offer the first time (or week) free to new students. There are many different places that offer yoga, most gyms, community centers, YMCA's and you should have no problem finding a local yoga studio offering classes in a variety of different styles and levels. You can also always find yoga videos online or on YouTube. Beginning a regular yoga practice, along with exercise, eating well and meditation will help round out your whole-body health and wellness routine.

Chapter 18

SLEEP AND PROPER REST

While we all enjoy being up and being active, rest is one of the most vitally important things we need to remember. We tend to run ourselves completely ragged. Burning the candle both ends, and as my mom likes to say for fun, you decided to light the middle just to see what happens. We get up and as soon as we get out of bed in the morning, we're off and running a mile a minute. It's go, go, go, go, go with so much to see and do, places to be and tons of tasks to accomplish until we 'crash' into bed at night. During the day we use things like caffeine and sugar to keep us going to make it to the end of the day because we always have *so* much to do.

This method works for a while, but the problem is we just keep getting busier and busier. We don't give ourselves a minute to think, let alone to rest and we certainly don't get enough sleep at night. This constant going, going, going can be extremely detrimental to our health and wellbeing. You end up sick and debilitated and it can end up taking twice as long for you to recover than if you had given yourself time to rest to begin with.

We need to practice both self-care and self-love with some time each day that is set aside for rest and relaxation. Doing something you love to do as opposed to something you're obligated to do. Something that will refresh and revitalize you. I'm not talking about mindless television watching either. I'm talking about time where you just do something that helps you to relax or calm down such as take a soothing bath, meditate, pray, and ponder the day or any issues you may currently have.

According to a study done by the Centers for Disease Control, nearly one-third of the population of the United States reported sleeping less than 7 hours per night (Liu, Y, et. al, 2016). Studies have shown that being sleep deprived has been linked to depression, ADHD, obesity, type 2 diabetes, cardiovascular disease, cancer and Alzheimer's. A new study recently published (Bellesi, et. al 2017) has shown that when you lack sleep, your brain literally starts to eat itself. While you sleep, your brain cells go to work repairing damage, cleaning house and removing waste and unnecessary memories. If you become sleep deprived, this can force the brain cells to go into overdrive and begin removing cells that are healthy and not in need to repair or removal.

The National Highway Transportation Safety Administration (Currin, 2018) has shown that drowsy driving mimics alcohol-impaired driving, increasing the risk of accidents and severely impairs decision making. There is an entire library of disasters that have been caused by sleep deprivation from the Space Shuttle Challenger explosion to the Exxon Valdez oil spill. Getting sleep is very important, yet we sometimes seem to think of it as being an inconvenient nuisance.

While I'm not saying these things could happen to you, I'm just making you aware of the real possibility that can come from being overly tired. It's important that you figure out what's best for you and go there. Dr. Deepak Chopra recommends trying to go to bed at 10:00pm and getting up at 6:00am, that will give you a solid 8 hours of sleep. Maybe 8 hours isn't long enough for you, or maybe it's too much. Each person is different, and you should try out a bunch of different times for sleeping and waking that make you feel the most refreshed. You can't fill from an empty cup and if you're not getting enough sleep, you're more on the empty cup side.

Action Step: For a week, set a hard time/rule for what time you're going to go to sleep. An hour before this time, make sure to remove all electronic devices from your field of vision. No TV watching, cell phones, tablets or eReaders, as the light emitted (even with the filters) can disrupt your circadian rhythm, making it more difficult to fall asleep.

During this time, I recommend you practice journaling and/or your chosen contemplative practice. In your journal, you can write down what you were grateful for that day, your thoughts and experiences for the day, and your intentions for the next day. It's during this time that you're prepping yourself for sleep. You could even take a bath, sit in a sauna or do a *light* bit of exercise for no more than 15 minutes to help put you into a deeper state of relaxation.

Remember that you are important too, so if you make the decision to set a specific time to go to sleep every night, let everyone know and also let them know that you are not budging from this self-care routine.

Chapter 19
ASKING FOR HELP

We are all busy with way more to do than we can ever get done in a reasonable amount of time. Some of us tend to take on more and more responsibilities because we feel as though it's our responsibility to do everything, to make sure that everything is taken care of. The problem is that we are only one person, and as such, we are only capable of so much.

What we should really do is focus on what we excel at (our zone of genius), and delegate the rest of the stuff that is just mundane, that we don't enjoy, or that takes up time we could better spend doing things that either bring us joy or make us far more productive. One of our biggest problems with this though is that we tend to think that if we ask for help, that it is a sign of weakness. We also tend to sometimes be slight control freaks and want everything to be done in a certain way.

What we don't realize though is that delegation is one of the most empowering things you can do and instead of being a sign of weakness, it's the sign of a great leader. It also empowers others (children, spouses, etc.). They understand that you care and trust them enough to get the job done. Also letting go of control takes the pressure and stress from you and it becomes ridiculously liberating to be able to let things go. You will be amazed at how many people are willing to help if you only ask.

When you delegate you also free up time that you can use to focus on what is most important to you, or far that all-important self-care. You can also swap with others if there is something you love to do that they don't and something they love to do that you don't it's a win-win for both people. You each get something out of the deal, and you don't have to do what you didn't want to.

Action Step: Find one thing that you do on a regular basis that you could either delegate, hire out or ask someone to help you with. Something that you do begrudgingly but do because you don't think that anyone else can do it. Something like cleaning, laundry, shopping, errands, small business tasks.

Give the tasks to someone else or hire someone to take on the responsibilities for you and then prepare to be amazed at how good you feel when you no longer must do everything yourself.

I have good friends who hired someone to do their laundry and grocery shopping for them. They found the experience to be extremely liberating because they no longer had to worry about whether they had food to cook for meals or what everyone was going to wear every day. I've recently hired a virtual assistant to help me in my day to day business tasks. She does things for me that I was doing before (and didn't mind doing), but those things took up a lot of time and by handing that work off to her, I was able to free up more time for myself to focus on the things that I do in my business that generate revenue for me instead of having to focus on the small, menial tasks that are necessary to run a small business. It's been one of the best things I've decided to do and now I don't think I want to function ever again without a support staff.

Section Three

NOURISHING SPIRIT MAINTAINING YOUR TRUE POTENTIAL

Chapter 20
LETTING GO

*L*etting go I have found to be the most difficult thing for most people to do. We all have this sense of self-righteousness when it comes to things like hurts and we hold on to them like precious jewels. We then do something unthinkable; we allow these hurts to define who we are. I have been abused, injured, insulted, neglected, and physically and sexually assaulted. We let these things take control of our lives and in turn, we give away all our power.

I am by no means by saying that these things aren't both traumatic and impactful. As someone who has lived with violence and abuse, and who has been sexually assaulted, I know how scarring and damaging these kinds of things can be. Growing up, we were also not well off, so as children, we were constantly ridiculed and picked on for having clothes that were dated, etc. These kinds of things can be traumatizing and leave long-lasting impressions on us that we just can't seem to get over, no matter how hard we try. These things should not be trivialized, but you should take a step back and see that by holding on to these hurts and these grudges, we are allowing the other person to win. Every time you bring up that old memory, you give away your power. You continue to be the victim, and the perpetrator wins all over again.

In order to get past these ills, we need to accept that they happened. They are done and there is nothing that you can do to change them. What you can do, however, is move on. Moving on and moving forward in your life and no longer allowing these things to define you, or to hold power over you, is one of the most liberating things you can do for yourself. Byron Katie says, "If you argue against reality you will suffer," and that is exactly what you are doing when holding on to these things. You are arguing with reality in asking "why" "how" or by saying, "I can't believe it!" By changing the story, you can change your life.

Dr. Wayne Dyer said, "When you change the way you look at things, the things you look at change". This is so true for letting go of old hurts and fears and doubts and limiting beliefs that we have held on to for so long! By changing the way you look at these past events, you can get clarity on the messages they were meant to convey and let them go because they no longer serve you.

Letting go also means letting go of the negative feelings that you have for yourself for the things that you have done. We are all our own worst critics, and if we had friends who talked to us the way we talked to ourselves, they would likely no longer be our friends. We all mess up. We all make mistakes. It is easy to sit around and beat ourselves up for doing whatever it was that we thought we did wrong or should have done differently. It's extremely difficult, however, to own our mistakes and to learn from them and then move on but move on and let go we must! It is all these little things we hold onto that cause us so much grief and heartache and why we destroy ourselves with things like food, drugs, and alcohol. We think that by letting go and forgiving that we're condoning the behavior, but we're not. Forgiveness doesn't mean you accept; it means that what happened doesn't control you anymore.

Action Step: I first came across this parable on Patrick Wanis, PhD's website (Wanis 2018)). It really made me think and I would like for you to do the following, read this Buddhist parable: Two Monks and a Maiden

Two monks (one old and one young) were travelling from one monastery to another. They were celibate monks, not even allowed to direct their gaze at women. After a long walk, they came to a river, which they had to cross. The river was flooded and there was no way that they would get across without getting wet. A lady was also at the banks of the river, wishing to cross; she was weeping because she was afraid to cross on her own.

The Monks decided to cross the river by walking through the shallow part of the river. Since the lady also needed to get to the other bank, the older monk, without any hesitation, picked the woman up and carried her across the river safely, and soon they reached the other bank, where he set her down. The lady went her way and the two monks continued their journey in silence. The younger monk was very upset, finding the older monk's kindness disturbing. As per their injunctions, they were not allowed to look at the woman, let alone touch her, and yet the other monk carried her all the way across the river!

After a few hours, the young confused monk couldn't stand the thought of what had happened which kept filling his mind, and so he began to berate the older monk, "We are not allowed to look at women, not touch them, but you carried that woman."

"Which woman?" replied the older monk.

"The woman you carried across the river!"

The older monk paused and with a smile on his lips, he said, "I put her down so long ago but why are you still carrying her?"

After reading this story, think about the things that you have been carrying? What are the heaviest burdens you bear? What can you set down to allow yourself to move forward more freely? Work on writing down all the feelings that are burdening you and try to work on putting those burdens down and just walking away from them. It's ok to tell them thank you for keeping you company for so long. To thank them for their part in making you the person that you are today. The person that can leave behind all the negativity, the strong and capable person who is no longer willing to be a victim. Be a WARRIOR!

Chapter 21
FORGIVENESS

*F*orgiveness is one of those things that we think of as letting someone get away with something or that by forgiving them, we are somehow condoning the wrongs that have been done against us. The problem is that the idea is false. Forgiving someone for something they did is to liberate yourself from judgment, fear, anger, and resentment.

What is anger? It is a punishment we give ourselves for someone else's mistake. Holding on to these hurts is detrimental to both your health and your spiritual wellbeing and development. By holding on to all the negativity, you are allowing that energy to fester inside of you like cancer and it will eventually destroy you. Forgiveness is not for the other person; it is for you. It is and a way for you to move past pain and anguish and to move into the glorious light of the beautiful healing energy of love. When you can look at your transgressors with love and compassion, then you have truly liberated yourself. Not only have you moved on, but you have reclaimed the power that you have allowed them to hold over you for all this time.

You also free up energy to move into positivity. Instead of being stuck in your negative story, you can move into the realm of possibility. By redirecting your anger to love and compassion, you shift the entire paradigm of your life. What you focus on expands, so forgiveness will help you to make room for more positive energy and possibility in your life. Always remember that hurt people hurt people and we need to be loving, forgiving and accepting of them for who they are and the lessons they are in our lives to teach us – only then can we truly be free.

Not only is it important to forgive others, but it's also important to forgive ourselves. We beat ourselves to death for perceived wrongs and it's a terrible way to spend your time. We all make mistakes; it doesn't help to dwell on those mistakes and keep rehashing them over and over in your mind. Forgive yourself. Be kind to yourself for doing the best thing you thought possible at the time. Sometimes we do things, even if we know (at the time) they are wrong, but we made the decision to do it so it's best to just say it happened and learn from that choice (and any consequences) and move forward. We cannot progress if we keep ourselves mired in the muck of the past.

For a long time, I was very angry and bitter about a lot of things that happened in my life. For the violence, abuse, neglect, ridicule, instability, hardships, racism, alcoholism and drug abuse that I experienced. I also hated myself for a lot of things that I did in my life and these negative thoughts and feelings of bitterness and anger turned into alcoholism for me. I drank to be able to sleep at night. I drank to quiet the thoughts running through my head at breakneck speed. I drank to forget all the bad things that happened in my life.

Then something interesting happened. I realized that my parents are who they are. I can't change them, but I can accept that they did the best that they could with the knowledge and resources they had. Regardless of how I was treated, or what happened to me in my life, I knew deep down they truly only wanted the best for me, even if they had no real way of showing me. This made it easier for me to shift my perspective. Instead of being angry that my mother was never around, I realized that she was away because she was working to put food on the table, and she wasn't always there for me when I needed her because she was wrestling with her own demons. This humanized her for me, and it made it easier for me to forgive her.

Forgiving yourself is another big one. For most of my adult life, I've never really felt worthy of all the wonderful things I have in my life because I've made some serious mistakes. Things that I've done that I was deeply ashamed of and also things I was terrified of people finding out about. I spent an inordinate amount of time beating myself up for the mistakes I've made in my life. When I finally came to the realization that I did the best I could at the time I made those mistakes with the knowledge that I had, it made it easier for me to not be so hard on myself. I was able to start letting go of all of the little things that I considered transgressions and through that process to start loving myself a little more each day.

As I forgave myself for what I thought were terrible things, I was able to see myself in a whole new light. I had been a wounded person and I was now doing the deep work to heal those wounds. I once had a bad fall; I fell off a ladder hanging lights around the holidays and ended up with what's called a deep bone bruise. I had no idea such things existed, but they do, and they take a very long time to heal. Mine took a little over a year for me to no longer be able to see the visible signs, but I could still feel the bruise. These deep wounds that I was working on were like the deep bone bruising on my leg.

After a few years, the visible signs disappeared (the drinking, the emotional eating), but the non-visible signs were still there (thoughts of inadequacy, depression) and through constant, vigilant mindfulness and meditation, I have been able to shift those thoughts and forgive myself entirely. I now love myself so very deeply because I understand that all those things that I went through were the necessary lessons that I needed to have in order to become the version of myself that I am today. I also realize that I will continue to make mistakes and as long as I learn from them, forgive myself and move on, I will continue to be the best version of myself.

Action Step: Think of something that you are holding on to that makes you angry every time you think about it. Now I want you to sit with that feeling for a minute. Think about the situation that occurred to bring about this result. Now I want you to think about the person or people who were responsible. Say to them in your mind, I understand that you were probably hurting when you said/did that to me. Say out loud to them, "I accept that, and I forgive you. I send love and blessings your way in the hopes that in the future you will make better decisions." Do this step multiple times, until the hurt feelings diminish, and you no longer feel the hurt, anger, bitterness or resentment. Forgiveness is something that takes time, but it is a cathartic process and a worthwhile one to perform.

Chapter 22

MEDITATION, PRAYER, AND CONTEMPLATIVE PRACTICES

Spending time in daily meditation, prayer or contemplation is perhaps *the* most important aspect for nourishing your spirit. By engaging in daily contemplative practice (whether it's meditation, prayer, or just plain old sitting in silence thinking of the meaning of life), you will continually deepen your connection to your Divine Self and, in turn, to Source. From this connection, you can gain insights on your life and the path you're meant to take that you otherwise would have missed.

We're bombarded daily with so much vying for our attention that it's necessary to be able to sit quietly and let all that go. When you do, you are freeing up the space necessary for Divine inspiration to flow through you. Now, a lot of people envision sitting in the lotus position and chanting "om" or trying to clear your mind of all thoughts. While this is a form of meditation, there are many others. People who are artistic can find creating art (painting, dancing, singing, drawing, etc.) as a form of meditation.

As such, repetitive things such as gardening, mowing the lawn, walking and looking for a specific thing on your walk (like purple flowers) are also forms of meditation. Then there is one of my favorites, coloring!!! I've used coloring books and crayons for many years to make me feel better and I'm glad that now it's become a more mainstream practice and you can purchase adult coloring books pretty much anywhere, and now I'm happy that I'm no longer the crazy middle-aged lady with the children's coloring books and the Crayola 164 pack of crayons who lies on the floor of her living room coloring. There is an immense selection of adult coloring books available and I highly recommend using them. By spending time focusing on performing these tasks, the outside world falls away and you are left with the space necessary for Divine Connection.

Action Step: Schedule time every day to perform some type of meditative or contemplative practice. Make it the second most important priority of the day, after movement. If you have a question you would like answered, think of the problem before you begin your practice. Ask yourself how best you should go about solving the problem. You will be amazed by the insights you gain while in contemplation. Ideas that just 'pop' into your head that you never would have thought of. People to get in touch with that could help you that you didn't even consider. These types of things are the types of solutions you will gain while in contemplative practice.

If you don't have a lot of time available, start off with this simple 5-minute meditation that I have done to help get you grounded and focused, and then you can work your way up to longer (insert link to meditation). I try to make it a habit to do small mindfulness and meditation breaks throughout the day. I have a timer set on my phone and I will work for roughly 90 minutes straight, then my timer will go off and I will get up from my work and wander around. Sometimes I'll just walk and think about a problem I'm trying to solve then I'll go outside for 10 minutes and look in the trees to see how many birds I can spot. I'll spend all my time outdoors trying to count birds (or bugs, or red cars, or something like that) to take my mind off all the racing thoughts. Once I am done and go back to my work, it's amazing how quickly I see solutions to my problems. You can download a few short, guided meditations from www.mindfulshift.org/bookbonuses.

Chapter 23
NATURE WALK, EATING, FOREST BATHING

Nature is something incredible. We live in such a magical, beautiful, and miraculous world and we tend to take it for granted. Not only do we take it for granted, but we also don't spend enough time in nature simply being and enjoying its majesty.

One thing that we don't really realize is just how beneficial for us to spend time in nature. To sit in the sand and have the waves lap at our feet. To spend time in the garden, digging in the soil with your bare hands, walking barefoot through the grass, spending time walking through the woods and breathing deeply the calm and peaceful serenity of the great outdoors. Feeling the sunshine upon your face.

Forest bathing, or Shirin-Yoku, has been a part of Japanese culture and a part of preventive medicine since the 1980s. When you spend enough time in nature, you begin to remember just how much a part of nature you are. How connected to the Earth, and in turn, how big a part you play in the world and just how important you are.

Spending time in nature can help reduce stress, eliminate fatigue, help with depression and anxiety, lower blood pressure, strengthens immunity, helps you to be more creative and helps to make you feel more alive.

One thing I consider to be the most restorative in my life is to lie in the grass and stare up at the sky, or under a tree looking up at the canopy of leaves. I love to get into my kayak and just float on the water and watch everything going on under the surface. I am an Advanced Master Gardener and I love going out and digging in the soil. To me, there is nothing that smells better than the scent of Earth as you're digging. Just being out in nature, in the peace and quiet where all you can hear is the rustle of your feet on the ground and the birds in the trees and the sighing of the wind through the tree canopy or grasses.

Action Step: Take some time once and week to spend time outside enjoying nature. Go for and walk and just look at nature. Don't talk on the phone or listen to music just be present and notice everything going on around you. Just two hours a week can help you to improve mental clarity, become more focused, help you be more creative and just feel better all around. Start out trying to spend 20 to 30 minutes a day outside in nature. If you live in a congested city, find a park that has trees, birds and animals or even some water. I know I always feel so much better when I'm near water or if I can watch fish swimming around in the water. I lived in the city for years and finally convinced my husband to move out to a more rural area and now that I'm out in an area that is less populated, I feel so much better. I sleep better, can concentrate more and am more productive. If you can't find time to get to a park, or outside to spend time in nature (I live in Michigan and there are parts of the year it gets so cold you can't go outside for long periods of time), try finding a nature YouTube channel and just listen to the sounds or watch a video of waves crashing against the shoreline.

Chapter 24

DEEPENING A SPIRITUAL OR RELIGIOUS PRACTICE

To me, cultivating a spiritual or religious practice is a great way to spend time. During that time, you will be able to clear away negative thoughts and feelings easier than you would on your own. When you spend more time deepening the relationship with source, you are in turn deepening your relationship with self. This can help you to gain insights and answers you normally wouldn't get from a standard day to day life.

We are all divine beings. All miracles and all connected to the same source, regardless of our beliefs. We all come from one and we all return to one. We come from nowhere to now here and then go back to nowhere. That nowhere is the source energy that flows through everything on this planet.

We are all connected to source at all times and no matter what anyone has told you, you are never alone, you are never separate and you do not have to do anything to be allowed to go back to source. Source is never-ending energy and you do not have to do anything special, be anyone special, believe anything special, or listen to anyone special to be able to connect to the truth that is always there and will be there for you, always.

Why is deepening this practice important? According to Psychology Today, positive characteristics of people who are spiritual are graciousness, compassion, self-actualization, and they flourish while taking the time to savor life's experiences. By deepening your practice, you begin to truly see your interconnectedness and realize just how important the small things in life really are. You will stop being bogged down by the mundane and begin to only do things that are truly beneficial to you. You no longer tolerate things that aren't necessary and, in that regard, begin to see much in your daily life that is unnecessary.

With all of this in mind, you will also begin to realize your importance in the world and begin to appreciate yourself and life more than you previously have.

One day I had what's known as a Satori moment, or what drunks call a 'moment of clarity'. I realized I was on a very dark path and needed to make a change or I would end up in a bad place, and I didn't want to do that. I love to read and one day shortly after quitting drinking, I found myself in a Borders Books (remember when those existed?) in Dearborn Michigan. I was walking in the self-help section of the bookstore, a section I have never previously been in before in my life (and I'm a book addict). I was just perusing the shelves and a book stood out to me. I don't know why it stood out to me, but it seemed like this book was calling me and I decided to listen to the call and answer. I picked up the book and started to leaf through it and really enjoyed what I was seeing.

While I was standing there, a bookstore employee happened to come down the aisle and he saw what I was looking at and he said to me, "if you really like that you'll enjoy this one too", and he pulled a book out and handed it to me. I decided I guess I was meant to have both of those books, so I went to the counter and bought them both. The book I picked up was The Tao of Health, Sex, and Longevity by Daniel P Reid and the book the employee handed to me was Siddhartha by Herman Hesse.

Now, I had already had a small taste of divine

wisdom in the ancient teachings of Marcus Aurelius in the form of his book, Meditations. I got that book totally by fluke (or not?) because I was in a history class my first semester of college. The professor gave us an assignment to write an essay and I happened to pick Marcus Aurelius. I got that book from the university library and fell in love with the wonderful philosophy. It's a must-have for any collection.

Now, back to the bookstore, those two books forever changed my life. Through reading and studying those two books, I learned how my mind and body were connected and how you can truly connect with self and in turn, source. Through the past 18 years of my sobriety, I have used the teachings I learned in those two books, and in subsequent years of studying all sorts of other materials, how to not only connect with the higher self, but how to work on self-mastery. This is something I will continue to do, likely until the day I die, so that I can continue to evolve and be the best version of myself possible.

Action Step: This is important, pick something that truly resonates with you. If none of these suggestions does, then do some research on other ideas to help bring you closer to the higher self. Some of the things you can do to begin to deepen your relationship with self are:

- Spending time alone, possibly in contemplation, prayer or meditation
- Yoga
- Going for walks or spending time in nature in some way
- Attend a faith-based service, preferably one that is inclusive of all
- Practice gratitude
- Mindful breathing
- Spiritual reading

Whichever of these you decide to try, begin to create rituals around what you are doing so that they become a part of your daily routine and eventually a habit.

Chapter 25
TEACHING AND VOLUNTEERING

What is the point of amassing all the knowledge you learn if you don't share it? Albert Einstein said, "It is the supreme art of the teacher to awaken joy in creative expression and knowledge." Sharing what you know, what you love, and what you are most passionate about can be one of the most rewarding things that you could possibly do in your lifetime. When you love something so much that you need to share with others how to do it too, that is the true expression of love.

The same thing goes for volunteering. Spending time in the community and helping can be both rewarding and beneficial. Beneficial not only to those you are helping but to yourself as well. Spending time volunteering and giving back can help to reduce stress, improve health and general overall wellbeing. By helping someone else out, you also begin to be grateful and see how fortunate you are because you are not where the people you are helping, or because you were there and made it past the hurdles and are now in a place where you can lead by example. You can say, "I did it, and so can you."

You can also increase your self-worth by helping others. We all have an innate need to be wanted and to feel useful so by volunteering, we're ticking off two of the boxes on Maslow's hierarchy of needs. Volunteering and teaching are things that I'm tremendously passionate about in my life. I create a mastery list every year instead of New Year's Resolutions and one year I decided to try the Master Gardener class. Now, this class is like a traditional college course, where it's 16 weeks and they go over a lot of material. They teach you just enough to be dangerous, but not enough to really do much good. They leave it up to you to go out into the world and make a space for yourself, or a niche.

The city I was living in at the time had a posting for the local library, they were looking for a Master Gardener to take over their butterfly garden and I just happened to see it (divine timing again?). I decided to volunteer for this, even though I didn't know anything about pollinator habitats at the time.

I signed up in the fall and had time over the winter to buy as many books on the subject as I could and ended up being the head Master Gardener for that location for 5 years. Unfortunately, I moved away from that city and after a few years of a long commute to and from the garden, I decided to give it up, but out of that, a passion was born.

I now spend my time volunteering to speak at garden clubs, community centers and conferences lecturing on building and maintaining pollinator habitats. I also work with neighborhoods, schools, and municipalities on designing and installing pollinator habitats. It's something that I truly enjoy, and I love passing on the knowledge to other people. I love answering the questions and getting knowledge from them to pass along to help other people. It's something that really makes me feel good and I know it helps the community, and pollinators, too.

Action Step: Think of some skill you have that you could teach to others or one place you could volunteer. It doesn't have to be a huge commitment, an hour or two a month and increase it if you have time and it makes you feel good. There is a great resource to help match you up to volunteer organizations looking for people in your local area, it's called Volunteer Match. You can go on, enter your information and it will tell you about local opportunities. You could find a local soup kitchen or food pantry, meals on wheels, or maybe volunteer at an animal shelter. Many shelters need help socializing animals and love having people on their lists to help walk dogs or play with kittens. How cool is that? You get to play with animals and help. I can't think of a better way to spend time. I love going to convalescent homes and spending time with elderly people. They get so lonely and just love having someone who's ear they can bend for an hour or two. You get to meet so many amazing people and they always have so much amazing information and history to share! Find something local to you that you feel like you could really get into and take some time to try it out. I promise you won't be disappointed once you realize the difference you've made in someone's life. Remember what Dr. Seuss said, "To the world, you may be one person; but to one person you may be the world."

Chapter 26
SPEND TIME CONNECTING WITH OTHERS

*H*umans are social creatures. We weren't meant to spend a significant amount of time alone and when we don't cultivate good relationships, we can feel like our life is lacking in some way. Also, the quality of people you spend time with is just as important. You want to surround yourself with likeminded people, or people whom you aspire to be like. The interesting thing about the quality of people you surround yourself with is that you will either rise to their level or sink to it, depending on the types of people they are.

It's important to spend time with people who challenge you, who make you laugh, who are always there for you (even if you haven't talked in a while). People who make you laugh and smile, who makes you happy, who accepts you for who you truly are without expecting you to be something you're not, and people who make you a better person. If you are fortunate enough to have friends like this, hold them as sacred. They are true treasures that nothing in the world can replace. If you have friends like this, try making time with them a priority. It doesn't have to be all the time, but it should be regularly. It isn't selfish to surround yourself with people who will either cheer you on or cheer you up.

By cultivating relationships, you are also creating your own community to which you belong. In that community, you find so many things, peace, a sense of belonging, strength, resilience, respect, self-worth, self-confidence, culture, and connection.

Action Step: Try to think of a few really great friends who you consider to fit the list of characteristics above. If you have three, you are very fortunate as a lot of people don't even have one. If you don't see those people on a regular basis, then try to schedule something regularly so you can get together and spend time with them. When you do that, make sure that you hold that time sacred. It is important that you hold this time sacred not just for your friends, but for yourself and your own wellbeing.

If you don't have any friends with the qualities

listed above, don't fret. You can still make friends, no matter your age. Go to networking events, find Facebook groups or go to Meetup.com. In Facebook groups or on Meetup, you can find people who have similar interests to you, and you can meet them in real life. I belong to a handful of local Meetup groups to express all my differing interests and it's always nice to find people to connect with on that level. Maybe you can meet people volunteering or teaching. There is no end to the places where you can find people to hang out with, the point is that you start looking. I have a group of girlfriends and we do Taco Tuesday once a month and get together to catch up for some good laughs, and good food. I wouldn't trade my Taco Tuesday's for a million dollars!

Chapter 27
PRACTICING GRATITUDE

There is so much in our lives that we take for granted daily. A home, job, spouse or partner, friends, boss, employee, co-workers, siblings, parents, children, service employees (such as wait staff, postal carriers, trash collectors, retail employees, etc.). We're so busy with our hectic lives that we forget to stop and be thankful for all the wonderful abundances that we have in our life.

We may think there is nothing to be grateful for because maybe there has been a lot of negativity in your life, but I'm here to tell you that even in those situations you can find something to be grateful for. I'm grateful to the men who abused me in my life because they made me who I am today. I know it sounds strange to say that I am grateful for this experience of traumatic abuse, but I truly am because without it, I wouldn't have come through the fire like a phoenix to share with you my experiences and to say that, "Yes, it happened and yes it was a horrible experience, but I survived and I'm better for it." I have much in my life that I could be hateful or spiteful for or even spend my days wallowing in self-pity, but instead every morning that I wake up I am so grateful for another day to be alive and to be able to use each day to try and be the best version of myself I possibly can be.

An interesting thing about gratitude too, the more you express gratitude for, the more abundance comes your way, so you truly have nothing to lose. What you focus on expands, so if you spend your time thinking about negative things, all the things you see or experience in your life will be negative. If you spend your time thinking about all the wonderful things you have and amazing opportunities that are there for you, more amazing and wonderful things will keep showing up. The funniest thing of all is that those opportunities are always there but with negative thinking, those opportunities are something that you would never recognize.

Action Step: Try starting a gratitude journal or gratitude jar. Try to write down three to five things daily in the journal or on little notes to put in the jar. I keep a gratitude journal by the side of my bed, and I write in it nightly at least five different things that I'm grateful for. I try not to repeat things, but some things I'm just so grateful for I can't help but repeat them. Things like sunshine, French fries, music, books, poetry. Try to think of something from the day that happened, that you saw or heard that you are grateful for. If something good happens to you, make sure to remember to write it down. Then, whenever you're feeling sad or down, you can look at some happy memories in the jar or in the journal to help you to remember just how awesome your life truly is.

Chapter 28
HUMILITY

Rick Warren once said, "Humility is not denying your strengths, but accepting your weaknesses," and C.S. Lewis once said, "Humility is not thinking less of yourself, but thinking of yourself less." This may sound interesting since I have been extolling the virtues of self, but humility is a very important characteristic and quality to work on. The best definition I found was in the Urban Dictionary:

> "True humility is to recognize your value and others value while looking up. It is to see there is far greater than ourselves into who we can become, who others can become, and how much more we can do and be.
>
> To be humble is to serve others and be for their good as well as your own.

> To be humble is to have a realistic
> appreciation of your great strengths,
> but also of your weaknesses."

Lao Tzu says, "When I let go of who I am, I become who I might be," and this is what is gained from humility. We all have such a strong sense of "self" and the labels that come with that like sister, mother, wife, daughter, husband, brother, father, employee, boss, friend. Mine is vegan. I've been vegan for more than 16 years now and it is a label that I hold onto vehemently. Being vegan is more than just a label to me, but sometimes I need to let that go and maybe see what becomes of me later.

Action Step: Try taking one of those closely guarded labels and see if you can let go of it for just a bit. Here's what I mean, say you're like me and you're a vegan. As a vegan, I do not condone the eating of meat or dairy products, or the use of animal products in ingredients. My husband, however, is not a vegan. For the longest time, it really bothered me that he wouldn't give up meat or dairy. No matter how much I preached, begged or educated, he has decided that being vegan isn't for him. A lot of other vegans give me flack for living with someone who doesn't adhere to the strict set of rules I have set for myself. I always tell them being vegan was my choice, not his and if he can go to bed at night knowing he did the best he could with what he knows then that's all that's necessary. It's not for me to make his choices or live his life for him.

So, sit down and have a conversation with someone who has opposing viewpoints with you on one topic or another and practice letting go of the need to be right and the need to control the outcome. All you have control over if yourself and if you can value other people and their opinions (even if you don't agree with them) you are well on your way to being humble.

Chapter 29
SELF LOVE

*I*t might seem ironic to follow up a chapter on humility with one on self-love, but that is exactly what I am doing. Now, taking those previously defined labels that we came up with in the last chapter, my bet is that in all those labels, not even one of them was "me" or "I". One of the main reasons for this is that because we spend all day wearing all these different "hats" (labels), we have no time for me/I.

We're mom, boss, employee, grocery shopper, dog walker, chauffeur, house cleaner, garbage person, child, parent, etc. In the shuffle of being all these different people to everyone else, we forget about us. We forget who 'we' are (if we ever really knew who 'we' were to begin with, that is). We think that if we take time to nourish ourselves, we are being selfish and taking away from someone else in return. This just isn't true. How many of us live lives that someone else planned out for us, or expected of us without even bothering to ask if it was what we truly wanted? This is something that is so universally unfair and it's not even close to being funny.

We marry people we aren't interested in, live in places we don't want to be, work in jobs that we hate, we spend our entire lives living for other people and never really experience the love, joy, and happiness that is our birthright. All because we feel a sense of duty or obligation to someone else for some reason. We neglect ourselves; we stop nourishing our lives and it causes that spark inside of us to dwindle until it's gone. We begin to hate ourselves for not having the courage to stand up to the people who proclaim to love us or have our best interest at heart we feel sick inside and have this empty, hollow feeling that we feel nothing will ever fill. We have to fill it with something, and those things sometimes end up being food, alcohol, or drugs, but even that doesn't work long term. It provides a temporary numbing to the pain and anguish. It's a vicious cycle, and it's time to end it.

There was so much in my life that I hated, most of all I hated myself. I had a deep sense of guilt and shame and I was humiliated because of what had happened with my life. I was literally destroying myself with food and alcohol because I didn't love myself. I didn't honestly know I was worthy of love because I had never really gotten much as a child. I now realize as I'm older and wiser that my parents did the best that they could with what they knew, and I love them for trying their hardest. Cycles repeat themselves and I was determined to put an end to this cycle. I finally realized I was worthy of love and through years of spiritual practice I've learned to truly love myself, my experiences, and my life.

I have also made a lot of changes in my life. I've removed all the negative and toxic people who were detrimental to my personal and spiritual growth and I've figured out what I'm meant to do and am working diligently on making that my reality. This book is the culmination of all of the years of lessons that I've learned and I want to use this knowledge to help you to learn your worth, to love yourself enough to let go of all of the negative things in your life. Pain is a catalyst for change and my pain was the catalyst for my life-altering changes and it's those changes that have brought me here to you right now, to help you move through the pain and the fear and the self-loathing to learn to truly love and appreciate yourself for the wonderfully divine creation that you are.

While you're at it, stop beating yourself up for

every single little thing. Every time you find negative words in association with self floating around in your head, be mindful of them and put an end to them. Stop being so self-critical and learn to love and accept yourself exactly as you are and stop trying to be something that you're not. Stop looking at advertisements that constantly tell you how bad your life is and how much better it would be if…if only you had this or went there or looked like that. You are perfection just as you are. The universe doesn't make mistakes, you are not a mistake and you, just you, are amazing. I know sometimes it's hard to believe that, but you are. If you're having a hard time with that, I recommend you try Louse Hay's Mirror Work.

Action Step: Find one thing you have been putting off doing because you're afraid of what your parents, friends, partner, etc. might think. Find one thing and just do it. If that's too scary for you (it's a pretty big leap), spend some quality time with yourself and use the time to discover the things that you really love and are passionate about. You can't fill from an empty cup, so spend some time finding what brings you joy that you can use to fill your cup. This makes me think about the movie, *Runaway Bride*, when Richard Gere's character confronts Julia Robert's character about the eggs. She always likes the same type of eggs that her fiancée at the time liked. I'm asking you now, how do you like your eggs? Are you so lost that you don't even know what kind of eggs you like?

Chapter 30
HAVE FAITH, SURRENDER, AND ACCEPT

*I*t might seem like an insurmountable task sometimes to just have faith that everything is going to work out. Especially when we want things to work out a specific way. We need to take a key from Abraham and put what we want out into the universe and then let go of the outcome. The best way I can think to express this is by listening to Garth Brooks' song Unanswered Prayers. Nothing I can think of puts it into such succinct words. Sometimes even if you have the slightest doubts, things won't work out.

We tend to obsess and become fixated on a specific outcome to the detriment of ourselves. The interesting thing is that when we become fixated, we feel the need to control the outcome. We neglect to see any other possible outcomes and opportunities. We constrict and narrow our focus so that when one door closes, we're so busy knocking on it waiting for it to open again that we miss the other doors that are opening. It's when we let go of the need to control things and letting go of a specific outcome that the true magic happens. It allows us to begin to see opportunities where previously none existed, well, they did but we were so clouded by our thoughts, fears, and desires that we missed them completely.

Say you're looking for a job and you're insistent that you make $$ this much money. Well, somewhere someone has an amazing opportunity that pays $$$ this much money. The problem is that you're so fixated on $$ this much money that you fail to see the $$$ opportunity, which would have been better for you in the end. I see this all the time with people, particularly small business owners. They become so desperate that they focus on the lack, and because they focus on the lack, they fail to realize opportunities that could help them out. One of my favorite movie lines (and I say it all the time to people) is from the movie *Super Troopers* where Policy Chief Grady says to Captain O'Hagan, "Desperation is a Stinky Cologne." I honestly can't think of a truer sentiment.

Acceptance is also another big one. We have

these expectations that things need to turn out a specific way and when they don't, we become upset, angry and sometimes ungrateful. We need to learn to accept that things happen for a reason and it's up to us to determine the reason and the lesson we are meant to learn from the experience. This will allow us to accept what has happened, that it happened, how it happened, even if it didn't work out the way that we anticipated or planned. Once you accept, you can move forward and progress a little more in your life.

In my life, a lot has happened that I didn't anticipate or plan. Let's be honest, we can't plan everything (even though I try hard to sometimes). I had some traumatic abuses at the hands of multiple men, these experiences left me wounded and scarred deeply. I was wounded, but I was also afraid. I was ashamed and full of guilt. Because of those feelings, I spent a good portion of my late teens and early twenties destroying myself and all my relationships. I was in a crazy downward spiral and heading towards a crash and burn. Then, something in my life changed and I began walking the path that led me here to you. It led me here so that I could share my triumphs and to let you know that everything really will be all right and work out in the end. It took a lot of surrender and acceptance on my part to get to where I am today and to be honest, I can truly say I'm grateful for all those experiences.

Action Step: My hope is that somewhere along this journey you at least had one item from each section that resonated with you. Not all sections will, and not everyone will see the same things in my words. I am hopeful that this book will help you to work toward healing your past traumas, help you to let go and surrender, to help you learn to be kinder, loving and more forgiving towards yourself, and at the end, you will come out a changed person. I hope that you will begin to implement the practices within these pages and begin to make them a habit that will help to make your life more whole, bring you joy, peace and harmony and best of all to help you connect with your highest self.

Finishing Up

While these few items only scratch the surface of the number of items you can do to help you better to connect to Self and Source, I include these items because I feel that they are the most important aspects to focus on and the easiest to incorporate into your daily life and maintain with relative ease. I want everyone to be able to feel the connection that there is between you, the real you, your mind and the universe. Once you realize this connection, then you will better be able to see just how you "fit" into this giant puzzle that we call life and once you realize where you "fit", then you can be better prepared to do what is your soul's true purpose. By doing this, you will be happier, healthier and more fulfilled than you could ever have imagined.

In order to create a more fulfilling life for yourself, it's important for you to realize just how much you matter and that your self-care is of the utmost importance. The saying goes that, "You can't fill from an empty cup, so take care of yourself first". This book gives you the tools, knowledge, and wisdom necessary for you to fill your cup first. Then once you have filled yours, you can spend time working on filling others. It isn't selfish to think first of yourself, even though we're trained to do so from childhood (and this is especially so for women). It is very important for you to learn that *you matter*, and by doing so you will begin to realize your full potential.

References

(1) Memory Changes in Older Adults. (2006). American Psychological Association. Retrieved October 20, 2017, from https://www.apa.org/research/action/memory-changes.

(2) Buckley, J. P., Hedge, A., Yates, T., Copeland, R. J., Loosemore, M., Hamer, M., . . . Dunstan, D. W. (2015, November 01). The sedentary office: An expert statement on the growing case for change towards better health and productivity. Retrieved October 12, 2017, from https://bjsm.bmj.com/content/49/21/1357

(3) Liu Y, Wheaton AG, Chapman DP, Cunningham TJ, Lu H, Croft JB. Prevalence of Healthy Sleep Duration among Adults — United States, 2014. MMWR Morb Mortal Wkly Rep 2016;65:137–141. DOI: http://dx.doi.org/10.15585/mmwr.mm6506a1

(4) Bellesi, M., Vivo, L. D., Chini, M., Gilli, F., Tononi, G., & Cirelli, C. (2017, May 24). Sleep Loss Promotes

Astrocytic Phagocytosis and Microglial Activation in Mouse Cerebral Cortex. Retrieved from http://www.jneurosci.org/content/37/21/5263

(5) Andrew.currin.ctr@dot.gov. (2018, December 18). Drowsy Driving. Retrieved January 10, 2019, from https://www.nhtsa.gov/risky-driving/drowsy-driving

(6) Wanis, P. (2018, April 19). The Parable of Two Monks & A Woman ~ Patrick Wanis. Retrieved July 7, 2018, from https://www.patrickwanis.com/the-parable-of-two-monks-a-woman/

Printed in the United States
By Bookmasters